INSIDE THE FOREST KINGDOM

FROM PECULIAR PLANTS TO INTERESTING ANIMALS

NATURE BOOK FOR AN 8 YEAR OLD
CHILDREN'S FOREST & TREE BOOKS

BABY PROFESSOR

EDUCATION KIDS

Speedy Publishing LLC

40 E. Main St. #1156

Newark, DE 19711

www.speedypublishing.com

Copyright 2018

In this book, we're going to talk about plants and animals that live in the temperate forest. So, let's get right to it!

THE THREE MAIN TYPES OF FORESTS

When we think of a forest, we think of an area that has an abundance of trees. But, there are actually different types of forests and they are different biomes. A biome is a community of animals and plants that occurs naturally.

There are three types of biomes that are forests. One of their major differences is where they are located.

- Rainforests are found in tropical areas near the equator where the temperatures are hot and humid.

- Taiga forests are found in the northern regions of the Earth where the temperatures are very cold.
- Temperate forests are located in the areas that are not too cold and not too hot. The word "temperate" means that it's a moderate climate.

TAIGA FOREST

Because they vary so much in terms of climate, these three types of forests have different types of plants and animals. In this book, we're going to talk in detail about the temperate forest.

PATH IN A TEMPERATE FOREST IN BRITTANY, FRANCE

VALDIVIAN TEMPERATE RAINFOREST

WHAT ARE THE CHARACTERISTICS OF A TEMPERATE FOREST?

There are four major characteristics of a temperate forest that distinguishes it from the other types of forests: its temperature, its seasons, the amount of precipitation it gets, and its soil.

Temperature

The temperature in a temperate forest is not as cold as the taiga and not as hot as the rainforest. In general, the temperature falls in the range of -20 degrees Fahrenheit and 90 degrees Fahrenheit.

MOUNT GULAGA TEMPERATE RAINFOREST

Season

Temperate forests have four easily identified seasons that each last about three months. In the spring, new plants pop out of the ground and trees grow new leaves.

Birds lay their eggs and mammals give birth to their new offspring. The summer is the warmest season, but it still doesn't get to the level of searing heat that is typical of the rainforest.

OAK FOREST TEMPERATE FOREST
VIEW FROM BELOW AT FALL

In the fall, the leaves turn beautiful colors and start to fall off. In the winter, there's usually snowfall and the animals can't find food as easily as they do during the other three seasons.

Precipitation

Most temperate forests have a great deal of rainfall throughout the year. They have as little as 30 inches of rain annually or as much as 60 inches of annual rain.

Soil

The soil in temperate forests is very rich with nutrients. Decaying leaves and other plant and animal matter creates deep, fertile soil that is perfect for the root systems of plants and trees.

AUSTRALIAN TEMPERATE FOREST

WHERE ARE TEMPERATE FORESTS LOCATED?

If you look at a globe and identify the landmasses that are located about halfway between the Earth's equator and the north and south poles, this is where temperate forests can be found. The eastern United States, Europe, eastern China, and the southeastern region of Australia are all locations with sizable temperate forests.

WHAT ARE THE DIFFERENT TYPES OF TEMPERATE FORESTS?

Not all temperate forests are the same. They differ in the types of trees that thrive there. The three main types are:

- Coniferous
- Broad-leafed
- A mixture of conifer and broad-leafed trees

LUSH TEMPERATE RAIN FOREST IN NORTHERN CALIFORNIA

A CONIFEROUS FOREST IN GERMANY

Coniferous

You can identify this type of forest because most of the trees are conifers. Conifer trees don't have leaves. Instead, they have needles.

Conifer trees have cones in place of flowers. For example, redwood trees and pine trees are two types of conifer trees.

Broad-leafed

You can identify this type of forest because most of its trees are broad-leafed. Broad-leafed trees are true to their name. They have large leaves that generally turn different colors during the fall.

Maple trees and walnut trees are examples of broad-leafed trees. Broad-leafed trees have flowers instead of cones.

MAPLE TREE

A mixture of conifer and broad-leafed trees.

This type of forest has a mixture of both types of trees.

PLANTS AND FUNGI OF THE TEMPERATE FOREST

There are three layers of plants in the temperate forest. The tallest trees make up the canopy and they block the sun from the plants below. The understory is the mid-layer. Small trees and shrubs make up this layer. The bottom of the forest floor is the layer that has wildflowers during the spring. Herbs and ferns grow at this lowest layer as well. They take advantage of the sunlight in the early spring since the trees haven't yet blocked out the sun with their fully formed leaves.

On the forest floor there are also many types of mosses and mushrooms. Wild mushrooms, many of which are dangerous to eat, are one of the most peculiar types of forest organisms. They look like plants, but they are really fungi. They are in the same category as mold and the yeast that bakers use to make bread rise. Fungi have an important role in the forest because they break down dead organic matter.

Many of the trees in the temperate forest are deciduous, which simply means that their leaves drop off as soon as the temperatures get colder.

The trees are bare in the winter and grow new leaves in the spring. Some types of evergreens keep their leaves throughout the winter months.

Certain species of trees, such as maple trees, use their own interior sap to assist them in surviving the winter months. The sap prevents their roots from becoming frozen. It's also used to provide a source of energy when it's time for new leaves to emerge.

RED MAPLE TREE COVERED WITH SNOW

A PACK OF TIMBER WOLVES

ANIMALS OF THE TEMPERATE FOREST

There are many different types of animals that live in the temperate forest. There are large predators, such as black bears and mountain lions. There are also mid-size predators like the red fox and the timber wolf. Deer munch the grasses or the bark of trees as they roam the forests and sometimes become prey for the larger forest predators.

COLORFUL TUCAN IN THE WILD

The forest is also filled with lots of small mammals, such as mice, rabbits, beavers, opossums, raccoons, squirrels, porcupines and hedgehogs. There are a variety of birds. Some birds, such as hawks and owls, are predators and will kill other types of birds as well as rodents.

There are thousands of different types of insects thriving in the forest. The forest is teeming with different forms of life. One of the challenges that forest creatures have is adapting to the change of climate, especially during the harsh winter months.

A PHYTOPHAGOUS BUG.
FAUNA OF RAIN FOREST IN ECUADOR.

In order to survive the winter and live until the following spring, animals have modified their behavior in different ways:

By remaining active

Many animals are active throughout the winter months. Some have a wide variety of foods they can eat. Others save up food so they can use the food during the winter. Some large oak trees have over 90 thousand acorns annually, so squirrels have plenty to eat as well as to store for the winter.

SQUIRREL

REDFOX

The red fox is another animal that is active all year round. The red fox is a predator with a varied diet.

By migrating

Many types of birds travel to a warmer location for the winter and return to the temperate forest when the weather improves in the spring. This type of relocation based on climate is called migration.

By hibernating

Some types of animals hibernate during the winter months. For example, the black bear gets fat during the summer and fall and then lives off its 5-inch layer of fat as it hibernates during the winter.

A LADYBIRD BEETLE LAYING EGGS ON A PINE NEEDLE DURING THE ONSET OF SPRING.

By laying their eggs for the next generation

Many types of insects don't survive the severe cold of the winter months. However, before they die, they lay their eggs. The eggs hatch once the weather gets warmer in the spring and a new generation of insects begins.

FOREST ANIMALS

Here is a sample of the many different types of animals that live in a temperate forest biome.

- The Black Bear
- The Beaver
- The Chipmunk
- The White-Tailed Deer
- The Red-Tailed Hawk

WHITE-TAILED DEER

The Black Bear

The most common of all the bear species in North America is the American black bear. The black bear goes into a period of hibernation in the winter.

To show its territory, it marks the trunks of trees with its sharp teeth and powerful claws. You don't want to come face to face with a black bear.

The Beaver

Beavers are semi-aquatic, which simply means that the live both on land and in the water. They eat the barks of trees and twigs. They also cut down trees with their very powerful front teeth. Their hind feet are webbed so they are good swimmers. Beavers are known for building lodges and dams.

The Chipmunk

If you see a chipmunk with very fat cheeks, it just means that it's carrying a bunch of food in its cheek pouches.

Chipmunks have a varied diet. They eat fruit, seeds, mushrooms and insects. They'll even eat bird eggs.

The White-Tailed Deer

The white-tailed deer is common throughout North and South America. It eats many different types of vegetation include shoots, grasses and leaves. It will even eat cactus plants.

RED-TAILED HAWK

The Red-Tailed Hawk

Because there are so many rodents living in temperate forests, red-tailed hawks can often be found flying above the treetops as they look for their next meal. These sharp-eyed predators also eat other types of small mammals, birds and insects. Red-tailed hawks are common throughout the North American continent.

SUMMARY

Temperate forests can be found around the world in locations that aren't too hot or too cold. They are filled with either conifer trees or broad-leafed trees and some have a mixture of both. There are various levels of plants in the forest. There is a canopy, an understory, and the lowest level, which is the forest floor. There are thousands of different animals, plants, and fungi living in every temperate forest.

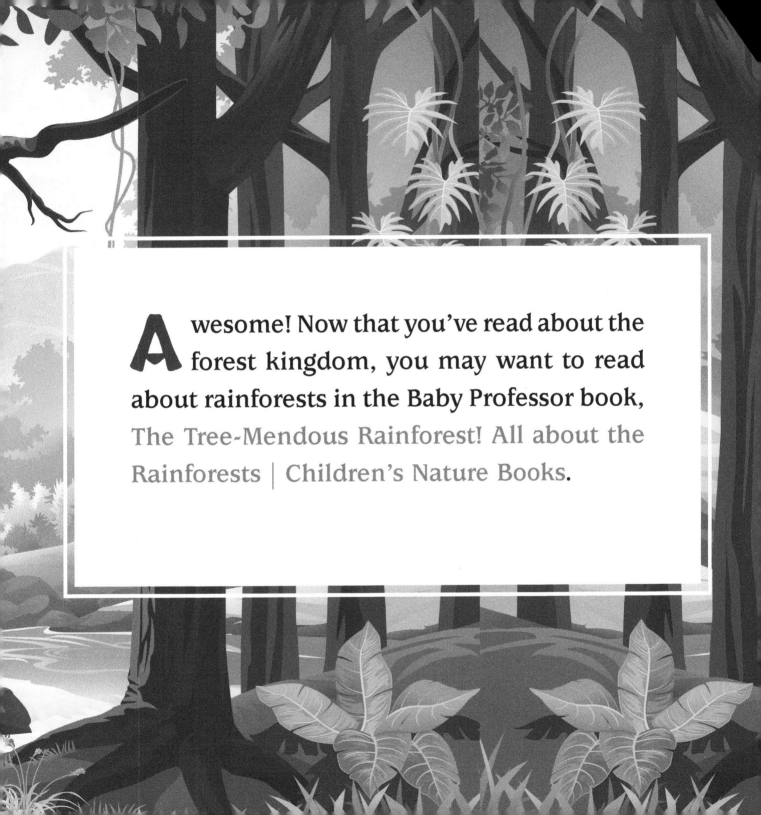

Awesome! Now that you've read about the forest kingdom, you may want to read about rainforests in the Baby Professor book, The Tree-Mendous Rainforest! All about the Rainforests | Children's Nature Books.

Visit

BABY PROFESSOR
EDUCATION KIDS

www.BabyProfessorBooks.com

to download Free Baby Professor eBooks and view
our catalog of new and exciting Children's Books